How To Move your Business From Chaos To Control

Three Simple Steps That Will Change Your Business Forever

John Millar

ISBN:1533315973
ISBN-13:9781533315977

DEDICATION

I dedicate this book to my mother and father, who
raised me while self-employed. They
taught me to work hard and listen to everyone but to
make my own choices as to what is right
and what is wrong.. and oh, did I mention work hard?

Anyone who tells you to work smart not hard hasn't
ever done it tough and realized that if
you work smart AND hard you will achieve more than
you can possibly dream.

CONTENTS

Profit Margins
Testing and Measuring
Delivery and Distribution

INCREASE YOUR PROFITS

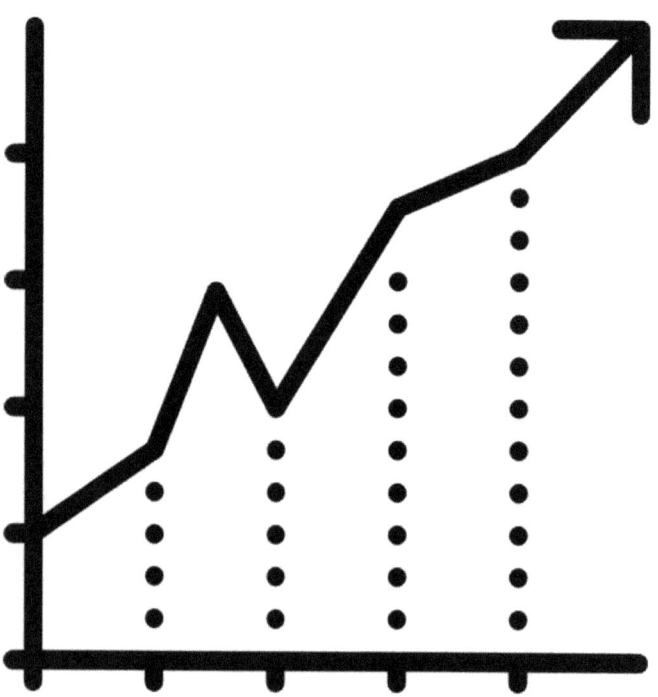

Increase Your Margins/Prices

This is as simple as it sounds – just hike your prices up 10% or so. This is good for most businesses, especially those in the service industry, where there are vast differences between the qualities of businesses. This allows you to make greater profit from each purchase made. Increasing your prices a little bit over a period of time should not upset your customers. It is possible that they will not even notice. Remember though, if you are in a highly competitive industry, where everyone advertises on price and it is always the customer's number one concern, raising your prices is not advised.

Sell More Big Margin Goods/Services

Move to products that offer more margins. This will work in industries where people are not particularly brand sensitive – that is, they do not care about the brand they use or buy. This may mean buying a slightly more expensive product that you can make a higher profit on. Quite often, a lower priced item will offer a greater margin. You should consider exactly how much each item makes you, and then continue to stock only those that make you the most money. If you work in the service industry, you should consider which services offer the most money for the least amount of effort.

NO Discounting

If you constantly discount, why have a regular retail price? This applies to businesses that are always discounting instead of coming up with decent marketing, or an actual reason to buy. Discounting not only costs you money, but it gives the impression that your normal prices are a rip off. Customers may also hold off buying, thinking that the item that is $100 today may only be $80 tomorrow. It is better to not discount and simply offer more add-on value. See the previous section for more information on adding value.

Sell Only Quality

Re-invent yourself as a quality dealer. Stop stocking the trashy lines and only sell the best. This will work when people care about quality (often, they care more about price and convenience) and want something better. More importantly, it will work if your customers have the money to spend.

By selling only quality goods and services, you can afford to increase your profit margins. Best of all you will not need to worry about customers bringing them back to be repaired.

When considering the move to higher quality stock, you need to keep two points in mind. First, the goods still have to be affordable for your existing clients. Second, you must be making more money from them on each sale.

Sell Your Own Label

This is guaranteed to increase your slice of the profits. Selling your own label also gives you the chance to discount on certain lines and undercut your competition. The beauty of this strategy is that because there is no intermediary, you are probably still making more profit than your competition would be at full price.

Sell An Exclusive Label

Start stocking a label or brand that your competitors do not have access to. Selling an exclusive label is important if your customers are price shoppers, yet also very interested in buying something with quality. Occasionally, people want something unique – if your customers are like that, this could be the way to go.

An exclusive label gives you the opportunity to increase your margin because your clients simply cannot go anywhere else to buy your product. Do not be too greedy. Only increase your margin as much as the market will bear. It is also important to remember that you may have to spend money to introduce the line to your customers – this may involve advertising and direct mail.

Sell Via Direct Mail/Internet
With the advent of the Internet, it is now possible to run a massive business from your bedroom using only a computer.

Sell Via Party Plan/Internet

This is an 'out of the box' way to sell your product. You do it in a similar way to Amway, or the party plan idea, such as Tupperware.

Keep An Accurate Database

This means that you ensure your database has the right names and addresses. This is important if you have a large database that you do not regularly check. It is especially critical if you base much of your business on mail order and direct mail.

If your database is out of date, you can waste a lot of time and money contacting inactive customers, or sending mail to an old address after your clients have moved. By regularly updating your database, you can be sure that your time and money is being well spent.

Commission Only Sales Team

One of the greatest financial burdens on any business is staffing. Holiday pay, insurance and sick days are all examples of wasted money that comes with paying wages. By employing sales people on commission only, you can avoid many of these unnecessary costs.

You have the added benefit of knowing that your team has to perform to survive. If they do not make sales, you do not pay them. This way you can be sure your company is not carrying any unwanted passengers.

Provide Team Training

This is as simple as it sounds, although the application is usually less simple – you have to commit time and energy, and so do your team.

Pay NO Overtime

There is no reason you have to pay overtime – if people are willing to work extra hours, great.

Reduce Team Size

This option is the last one most business owners want to explore – it means hurting people's feelings, putting them through hardship. If your business is over-staffed, you simply have to reduce the team number, or you are not giving yourself a fair chance to profit. Moreover, regardless of how much you like your employees, remember, you started the business for you.

By evaluating your systems, you may be able to reduce the size of your team without losing productivity. In many cases, you will find that some members of your team have long periods of inactivity during the day. By eliminating some of your team, you can get the most out of those remaining, and cut down on your wage expenses.

Reduce Unnecessary Management

It is a common mistake to beef up the area of 'middle management'. Let people manage themselves. If they do not get the work done, they are out! Taking away unnecessary 'watchers' can also make your team more responsible – they start to believe that you trust them, and they will live up to your expectations.

Improving your team training can assist in this area. Many modern businesses suffer from top-heavy staffing levels. By putting systems into place and improving the training of your team, it may be possible to make some of the management positions in your company obsolete.

Reduce Directors Fees

Simply stop paying yourself so much. This is never the 'fun' option. Many directors draw excess money out of their companies, which eventually creates cash flow problems.

It is important to have a pool of money so you can pay any unexpected costs that arise, or take advantage of investment opportunities. It is better to wait until you feel you are in a strong enough financial position before you start taking a high wage out of the business. It is a small sacrifice in the short term, which will no doubt pay off in the long term.

Efficiency, Productivity & Time Management

These three areas can be responsible for large sums of wasted money. If you evaluate each of these areas individually, you can quickly identify which of them is costing you money.

Notifying your team of the minimum performance standards that is expected of them can help to fix any problems. It is time to get a bit tougher – think about what is possible. What could the best employee achieve in a day? There is nothing wrong with asking your team to work at that level. It is funny – when you ask more of people, they tend to find a way to stretch and reach the next level.

Negotiate Employment Agreements

Have a contract that you and your team members sign. Savings can be made quickly. Eliminating overtime and holiday loading are examples of achievable goals that can be successfully negotiated. It is important to remember that in order to attract and keep good people; you must offer them something worthwhile. You need to have a pay-off in some other area – perhaps you could offer someone the same pay rate without sick pay, but with an extra day off every week. You also need to investigate the legalities.

Team Incentives Based On Margins

Offer your team an incentive if they get the highest possible margin on items. This is excellent for businesses where staff have a tendency to make deals in order to win the business. It is also a good idea if you sell inexpensive, low margin product and very few high quality items with good margin. An example of this would be if you had standard and discount prices.

Simply pay your sales team a higher commission on anything that they sell at full rate. Why should you be the only person concerned with margins? Your team can assist you in boosting your margins, particularly if you make it worth their effort.

Reduce Duplication

By cutting down on duplication and unnecessary paperwork you can save your company hundreds of dollars. It is a common story – many business owners, in an effort to really get things systemized, overdo it – they have a form for this, which goes into a file, and then a record is made here, which is made in triplicate over there, then entered into the computer. Keep it simple – think of things in their least complicated forms. The customer buys something, they get a receipt, and you keep a record. Maybe you can find a way so that everything is taken care of at the time of sale. Take some time to look at your existing systems to see if there are any areas guilty of duplication. This can eliminate wasted time and expense.

Know Your Actual Costs

Do you really know how much things cost you? More than likely, everything costs more than you expect. Many of your expenses are never evaluated. If you take some time to find out your actual costs, you can then look at ways to reduce them. By getting quotes on different services and products, you can save substantial amounts of money. There is nothing wrong with shopping around and finding a better deal on everything – you will find one.

Work Costs As A Percentage of Sales

Calculate all costs that arise in your business as a percentage of sales. This gives you an idea of how many sales you need to make before you start showing a profit. To do this, work out how much it costs you to run your business every week. You need to include all expenses, from wages to stationary, electricity bills to rent – anything that you have to pay to keep your doors open. Then work out how many sales are needed to cover that cost before you start to see a profit.

This may also tell you if your business has a chance of success, or if you are really kidding yourself. Once you have identified this figure, explain to your team what is required to keep the business profitable. This will motivate them to increase sales and achieve their goals.

Set Monthly Expenditure Budgets

Set a budget for the month, and do not go over it, regardless of the circumstances.

This is important if your business is to remain viable. By setting monthly expenditure budgets and sticking to them, you can make sure that you are never in the situation where your company has more money going out than it has coming in.

Of course, if it is impossible to set your budget lower than your expected income, you need to ask yourself what is going wrong. You need to also remember that sometimes you have to spend money to make money.

Allow Your Team To Buy Only With An Authorized Purchase Order

Use a purchase order system – your team members need to fill one out and have it authorized before they buy anything. This way you can then keep track of any money that is being spent and allocate in advance to the proper category.

This is necessary to ensure that your money is only being spent on the bare essentials. It can slow things down, especially if you are not present every day and every minute. Usually, this is a small inconvenience for the benefit.

You may be surprised by how much money is

wasted in your business. Employees often do not understand business as well as you do, and may not be aware of precautions needed to keep your business profitable.

Better Negotiation Skills

The first step to developing better negotiating is to understand what the other person wants – if you know this, you can work out how to give it to them, and still get what you want. You need to be strong in this area if you want to get the best deals. Everything from employment agreements to negotiating with your suppliers depends on your skills in this field. Rehearsing in front of a mirror or practicing in the car as you drive can help you develop these skills. You need to make sure you are getting the best deals from your suppliers so that you are making the maximum profit from selling their products.

Reduce ALL Costs By 10%

It is not easy but with a bit of effort, it is possible to reduce all your costs by at least 10%. The best way is to sit down with your team or business partner and run through every cost you have in your business. Think of at least two ways to reduce every cost by 10%. Once you have thought of a suitable way, make a commitment to do something about it and create an Action Plan. Lower overheads mean greater profits, so you need to devote some time to this area.

Think outside the box – how is it possible to cut every cost by 10%?

Do It Right The First Time

You are only paid to do most things once, so if you do not do it right the first time, your profits can quickly dwindle.

Recycle

This is exactly what it sounds like – re-using things so that you do not have to buy them again.
There are many different products you can recycle to help reduce expenses. If you have a photocopier, then use both sides of the paper, or buy refillable ink cartridges for your printer. By making the effort to recycle, it is possible to save a considerable amount of money over a period of time.

Decrease Range

Stop carrying things that are not making you any money – start to specialize in just one item ... the one item that people buy. The longer an item sits on your shelf, the less profit you will eventually make from it. If you eliminate your slow moving stock and only carry those lines which sell quickly you can make more money per item sold.

Have a closed-door sale to get rid of all the excess stock you have accumulated over the last year. Sell it all, generate a bit of cash flow, then start just stocking the good stuff.

Take Stock On Consignment

More and more suppliers are willing to let you have stock on consignment. With more competition, they have to go the extra mile. This way you do not have to outlay money on stock that could take some time to move. You do not have to pay for it until it sells which means that your money can be working for you elsewhere.

This is one of the most effective ways to increase your margins. Of course, it is important that you give the consignment stock the same attention as the paid for stock. There is no point even getting it in if you think: "Oh well, I have not paid for it, who cares if it sells?"

Lower $$ Tied Up In Inventory

You should never have too much stock in inventory. This has an adverse effect on cash flow and you run the risk of being stuck with it if trends change.

Always keep your inventory as low as possible, without running short and then order stock only as you need it. It is important to run your business lean and mean – if that means you are occasionally inconvenienced or waiting on something, then so be it. The benefits will more than compensate.

Sell Only Fast Moving Stock

Make a commitment to just sell stock that you already know is popular. Any stock that sits on shelves is wasting money. The longer it sits there, the lower the margin you make on it when it finally goes. If the stock is particularly slow moving, it will probably need to be sold at a discounted price.

Buy In Bulk, Pay & Receive Over Time

Order a large amount, thus taking advantage of a bulk buy deal. The trick is, you pay over a series of months, and only receive a little bit at a time – most wholesalers are happy with this arrangement. You have made a commitment to keep buying from them, and they only send you what you have paid for.

Manufacture Yourself

If you are selling a lot of a particular item, you should look at the possibility of manufacturing it yourself. Obviously, the benefit of making it yourself is that you make the maximum profit out of each sale. Instead of your manufacturer making a lot and you making a little, you get both slices.

This strategy is one well worth looking into, especially if your product is simple to put together, and you are quite certain you can make it without loss in quality.

Repackage Smaller/Own Label

Reduce your packaging, and start doing things in a minimalist way. A lot of your profit can go into the packaging of your product. By reducing the size and amount of packaging on each product, you can save quite a bit of money.

To further increase the amount you make on each sale, shop around to get quotes from different packaging companies.

Promote Idle Time

Think of something productive you can do with the time you have free. If your business is service-based, then this is an area you may need to look at. For companies such as plumbers, mechanics or accountants, who make their money from charging an hourly rate, promoting idle time is critical. To get clients coming in during quiet periods, you should look at offering a reduced rate or additional free service. To operate during these times at a slightly reduced fee is better than not operating at all. You could also start another enterprise – maybe even a secretarial service, where your staff does typing in between taking phone calls and servicing clients.

Rent Idle Space

If you have an office, warehouse or workshop space that is not being used, you should be trying to rent it out. In many cases, it is worth the time and expense of renovating the area to make it more attractive. This gives you extra revenue and can be great for business if you get a company in that provides a service that complements your business.

Work Two Or Even Three Shifts

This is a great idea for any business looking to cut down on the amount of equipment they need to purchase. For example, a data entry company could run two shifts rather than buying two lots of computers. This eliminates the need to pay overtime as well as saving you money on equipment. This will not work if your business is based around customers, and cannot operate when they are not calling. If you run a business where one half of your team service and the other half deliver, you could have the sales team in your office in the day, and the delivery team at night – that means half the office space.

Have Smaller Outlets

Ask yourself if your business could operate in a smaller space. If you have excess floor space then you have one of two options. You can either rent the unused space to another business or move to smaller premises. If you are paying for floor space that is not being used, then moving will save you an unnecessary expense. Naturally, you need to also be thinking about the future – will you be expanding and needing more space to service all those extra customers you get from applying the ideas contained in this guide?

Work From Home

Could you run your business from home? Many people believe that when they go into business for themselves they must rent an office or a shop front. The truth is that many small businesses can be run from home.

This cuts down on your overheads and transportation costs, as you do not need to commute to work. You also have the added advantages of paying only one lot of bills and receiving a number of tax benefits. Therefore, if working from home is an option, then you should take advantage of it because lower overheads mean greater profits.

Have A Mobile Business

This can be a great one for mechanics and

hairdressers in particular. As with working from home, having a mobile business dramatically reduces your overheads. It also offers similar tax benefits and is often more convenient for your customers.

Join/Start A Buying Group

If you are aware of a Buying Group, join it. If not, start your own.

By joining with other companies to form a buying group, you can achieve substantial savings in a short period of time. The idea is quite simple. Manufacturers offer bulk prices to companies that buy a lot of stock. As individual companies, you probably cannot buy a large enough volume to get these prices. However, if you join other companies that also sell these products, your combined purchasing power should enable you to get a better price.

Re-finance

If you have a number of loans, then you need to consolidate them into one. This gives you the advantage of only paying off one interest bill.

You will need to shop around to find the best interest rate. This does not always mean the least expensive, so make sure the one you choose suits your particular needs.

With banks becoming more and more competitive, there is always a bank out there willing to provide you with a loan for less. If your bank is not willing to match their rate, shop around.

Charge For A Finance Facility

Any business that offers finance for customers should arrange it on a commission basis. Approach a number of loan companies and offer to sell their product for a commission. This is a great way to increase your profits from each sale. You can also charge interest on 30, 60 or 90-day accounts. To hide this extra charge you simply offer a discount for accounts paid within seven days. This means that any account that is not paid in that time has interest attached.

30 Day Terms To 7 Days

Change your accounts from 30 to 7 days. Also, change your policy so that overdue accounts accrue interest and extra charges.

This allows you to make a few extra dollars – people will usually miss the seven-day period. They will understand they are being charged more because they did not pay on time. You should make sure that your service is up to scratch though – this could seriously annoy people, and if they can, they will go somewhere else. If your business is special, customers will be happy with the new terms.

Invest In Technology

If you are going to buy something, why not buy something that will mean you can produce more in less time and with less expense? This will improve the speed at which your business operates.

You need to have the fastest, most reliable

machines that you can afford. You should also have all your accounts and files on computer. To manually do any bookkeeping in this day and age is criminal.

Systematize The Routine, Humanize The Exceptions

This means that you should put systems in place to cut down on your team's workload. Effective systems can often make the people that were performing those tasks obsolete. Anything that cannot be systemized needs to be run by people. However, always look at putting a system in place rather than employing more people. A system means that things are done consistently, regardless of the staff member.

Automate As Much As Possible

Investing in machines to do the work previously done by a team member is a wise choice. By automating, you not only save money on wages, you can also increase your productivity.

This means that your goods will cost less to produce and therefore give you a greater profit margin. If there is a way to automate, look at the costs involved to see if it is worthwhile. Remember, machines do not make mistakes (usually) and can work through the night without needing overtime.

Sell Obsolete Equipment/Machinery

Offload anything that is outdated and almost unusable for your business. Printers and dry cleaners are notorious for keeping outdated pieces of equipment. Any old piece of machinery that you have should be sold to generate extra revenue. The profit from the sale of old equipment can be used to offset the cost of a replacement.

Reduce/Eliminate Taxation Expense

For this, you need to find an accountant who is financially literate. And no, just because they are qualified as an accountant does it mean that they know how to reduce your tax expense.

A top accountant can minimize or eliminate your tax burden, so it is worth taking the time to find one. It is also important to find an accountant who plays 'on the line' – that is, they know the law and recommend strategies accordingly. However, they also know how to walk the line to get the maximum benefit. Of course, you do not want to be too flamboyant – you will attract an audit and no one wants that.

Negotiate Fixed Not Variable Expense

If you use a particular service on a regular basis, then you should consider arranging a fixed rate. For example, if a business needs to have its computers serviced four times a month, and the fee is $120 per service, it would be worthwhile arranging to pay a retainer of $160 per month and $60 per service. This can be applied to any regular service you use.

Employ People In House

This is a great way for you to reduce your expenses and increase your margins. In many cases, it is far less expensive to pay somebody a wage than it is to sub-contract the work out. Of course, it is a question of finding someone who can produce the same result, but is willing to work for one business.

Outsource

It is not always less expensive to employ someone in-house. If you do not have enough work to keep them busy full-time, or if the cost of the equipment they need is too great, you are better off outsourcing the work.

Use A Company Card For Bonus Points & Up To 55 Days Interest Free

Use a company credit card rather than paying by cheque. This way you can leave the money in your account for up to 55 days earning interest, or direct it into other investments.

Using your credit card can also gain you bonuses such as Air Miles Points. These points can be accumulated and then used later for business trips. Most suppliers will be just as happy (if not happier) to accept credit cards, and it also makes payment over the phone possible.

Rent For Maximum Tax Write Off

Renting is a great way to gain tax exemptions. If you own the building you work in, it will be classed as an asset and cannot be claimed. However, if you rent the building it becomes an expense, which can then be claimed. Saving money on your tax will naturally help make your business more profitable.

Change Accountants

This is quite simple – you simply find another accountant. Get the new one to write a letter to your current accountant and notify them that you have changed. Not all accountants are financially literate. You need to find the best accountant in your area. A good accountant will cost you a lot of money, but they will also save you a lot. Ask friends who they are using and if they would recommend them. Ask potential accountants what they can do for you that your current accountant is not doing.

Keep Overheads To A Minimum

This can be as simple as turning off any unnecessary lights, or re-negotiating your rent. You need to look at all areas of your business to find potential savings. With the deregulation of many industries, you can save money on things like electricity and phone expenses. Wages are another area where substantial savings can be made. Consider hiring salespeople on commission only, or negotiate a more suitable employment contract.

Stop Running Ads That Do Not Work

If your ads are not making you money then you must stop running them. You should only run ads that immediately make you money. It is important to test and measure each ad to make sure that you are getting the maximum return possible. When you find one that works, keep using it. Of course, this only comes after a significant period of testing and measuring – it may be 6 months before you find the right ad. Unfortunately, expenses can add up in the meantime. You could still look at this outlay as an investment – it is an investment in finding out what works and creating that magic ad.

Measure Everything

Measuring and uncovering your true business numbers needs to be applied to all areas of your business. Everything from your advertising to the amount of phone calls you make needs to be tested and measured. When you test and measure every area of your business, you can start to identify ways to cut costs and increase profits. If you do not know exactly how much you are spending and how much you are making, you will not have a clue where your business can be improved, and you may end up spending money in an area that is draining your funds.

Regular/Timely Accounts

Send out 7-day accounts as soon as the job is completed or the product has been delivered. Do not wait until the end of the month. The money is always better off in your account than theirs, so get your invoices out and follow up. Do not let people get away with not paying – charge them extra fees and interest for late payment. It may annoy some people, but it is possible you do not really want those customers anyway – they end up being more trouble than they are worth.

Get Phone Bills Etc. Checked

Do not assume that your bills are correct. In many cases you can save $$ by checking your bills to find out if you have been over-charged. Someone must check every bill, and then follow up on discrepancies.

Keep your own records if possible, and check every bill against them. You may be surprised by how much you are being over-charged, and it may make you reconsider who your suppliers are.

Test & Measure
EVERYTHING

www.moreprfitlesstime.com | www.ceo-ondemand.com.au

Complete & Keep To Monthly & Yearly Budgets

Poor Cash Flow is what usually kills business. Know where yours is going as regularly as possible.

The key to ensuring your business maximizes its cash flow is to complete and stick to regular budgets. Budgeting makes sense. It is good business practice. It also allows you to keep your finger on the pulse of your business. If you regularly monitor your cash flow, you will have early warning of impending problems. If cash flow is down according to budget, you need to take immediate action Otherwise, your business will run into serious trouble. If cash flow is up, you can divert surplus funds into areas where it can better work for you.

Remember, if you are not concentrating on creating cash flow, then you are wasting your time in business.

Measure Conversion Rate for Each Sales Person

By measuring conversion rate, you will know where you have to improve and exactly how you are performing.

The conversion rate is the difference between those customers who could have bought from you and those that did. If ten people come into your shop or enquire about your service and only two buy, the conversion rate is two out of ten, or 20%. Knowing what the conversion rate is for each sales person allows you not only to devise plans to increase it; it also allows you to work out how the business is performing and what its potential is. If you are getting by with a 30% conversion rate, imagine how your business would run at 70%.

Keep A Record Of Your Profit Margins

Know what your big margin products and services are and focus on them. It is not just about turnover, it is also about profit.

Remember, profit is king. You need to know which products or services bring in the most profit because it usually takes just as much effort to sell highly profitable items as it does to sell something with low profit margins. Concentrate on what is good for the business first – then the less profitable items will be the icing on the cake.

Complete A Petty Cash System
You do not have to write a cheque for everything, but be sure to keep receipts.

It is all about being in control of your cash flow. Develop a simple system that allows you to issue petty cash when needed. You can appoint someone responsible for this function. Issue them with a receipt book and decide on a procedure, then let everyone know.
Complete A Purchasing System For All Internal Purchases

Do not let anyone spend money until they have an authorized purchase order. Create a simple system for this.

If everyone is allowed to go out and make purchases

whenever they want to, you will have no control. Not only will you be losing the opportunity to negotiate better prices with suppliers based on volume, you will also be losing control of your cash flow. People might be tempted to buy more expensive items, as they may not be aware that inexpensive ones could do the job just as well. Duplication is sure to occur, resulting in higher expenses and a negative impact on your bottom line.

Always Complete A Marketing Campaign Profit Analysis

Know where you are making money and where you are losing it.

If you spend money on marketing, do you know it is working? Do you have any idea how much every new customer costs you? Do you know how much you are losing to make that first sale to a new customer? Moreover, do you know when that customer becomes profitable to you? One simple way to find answers to these fundamental questions is to analyze your marketing campaigns. You need to compare the total cost of the campaign with the number of new customers it brings in.

Develop a simple questionnaire or get each sales person to ask some questions and keep notes. Then record each purchase. This will allow you to analyze whether you are making a profit or losing money. You can then fine-tune your campaign, drop it or keep running with it.

Continuously Measure The Number & Origin of All Leads

The more you know, the easier it is to make decisions about what is working and what is not.

Few businesses know how many leads they get each week. Even fewer know where those leads came from. Develop a database and keep in regular contact with them. Work on converting these leads to customers.

If you get the same number of leads, whether you run a marketing campaign or not, you need to rethink your campaign. However, you will never know what to fix if you are not continuously measuring the number and origin of the leads you get.

Constantly Monitor Credit Control & The Age Of Your Accounts

You are not a bank, so do not go loaning people money. Give them an incentive for early payment.

If you monitor the age of your accounts, you will soon see which ones pay on time and which are getting very overdue. Remember, the name of the game is cash flow. If the cash owed to you is not coming in regularly or when due, it will be to the detriment of your business. It will be costing you money. Work on getting money owed in when it is due, even if this means offering incentives. These could amount to a small percentage discount for prompt payment. The cost of this to you could far outweigh the consequences of having large amounts of money outstanding.

Measure Your Average Dollar Sale For Every

Team Member

Know who is making the money and who needs training.

Knowing what the average dollar sale is for your business as a whole will allow you to quickly and easily keep your finger on your estimated profit. It will give you an insight into what needs to be concentrated on to increase the overall profitability of your business. It could be as simple as increasing the average dollar sale for each team member.

This is also an excellent indicator as to who could benefit from training or retraining. It could not be easier.

Record The Number Of Transactions For Each Customer

If they are coming back then it is a great thing to know and measure.

A simple system will tell you how many times each customer buys, when they buy, what they buy and how much they spend. This data will prove invaluable for future marketing campaigns. It will also be invaluable in your efforts at building customer loyalty. Remember, hanging onto an existing customer is far less expensive than finding new ones.

Complete A Monthly Balance Sheet

Know your worth and whether the picture gets better or worse every month.

A monthly balance sheet is a snapshot of the health of your business. It will tell you whether the things you are doing are working or not. It will tell you whether you need to be thinking about doing things differently. Moreover, if you are building up your company, the monthly balance sheet is an excellent indicator of the rate your company is growing at. It is also an early warning tool, indicating looming trouble. Use it.

Measure Key Performance Indicators In All Areas Of The Company

You cannot manage what you do not measure. Make sure everyone measures his or her Key Performance Indicators.

By doing this, you will also be ensuring people aim for, and achieve, their own individual goals. This will not only have positive effects on the running of your business, it will have positive effects on your team members as well.

Complete A Weekly Bank Reconciliation

Know you are on track with your accounting and that the bank is doing a good job.

Reconciling your bank account on a weekly basis allows you to quickly pick up any errors or misallocations that could be costing you money. It will help pinpoint mistakes due to internal record keeping, allocations, or pricing. You can then tighten up on the appropriate system.

Weekly reconciliations also allow you to monitor your cash flow.

Daily Or Weekly Update Your Cash Flow Statements

Cash flow is what usually kills business after business. Know where yours is going as regularly as possible.

If you have good systems in place, you should know what your cash flow is doing. By updating your cash flow statements on a daily basis, not only will you have the very best information available, it will also save you time and effort. It is much easier entering a few transactions on a daily basis than a large amount weekly or monthly. There will be fewer errors, too.

The sooner you get warning of a looming cash flow crisis, the sooner you can make plans to avoid it. You will be more in control of your business and able to direct its growth according to your overall plan rather than having to spend time sorting out crisis after crisis.

Have A Daily Banking System

Get your money into the bank with 100% accuracy as soon as possible.

That way, not only will it be safe, it can also start working for you. Furthermore, banking on a daily basis involves less accounting in the end and ensures there is less chance of mistakes. Cash in the bank equals cash flow. Your bank manager will love you.

Complete Regular Stock Control Check Ups

As an accountant, you have to make sure the numbers are always accurate.

It is far easier to measure small amounts on a regular basis than a large amount occasionally. Errors due to fatigue, confusion and boredom can easily creep in if you handle one massive stock control check-up each year. More frequent check-ups also act as early warning signs and can point to existing or upcoming problems.

Complete All Regular Government Returns

Nothing will hit harder than a tax return not filed or paid on time. Make sure either you or your accountant follows this through.

If you are conducting regular stock control checkups, completing monthly balance sheets, reconciling regularly with your bank, and keeping on top of your cash flow statements, you should have no trouble completing regular tax returns on time. Build this into your system, and include it in your bookkeeper's (or other responsible person's) Key Performance Indicator. There should be no excuse for not meeting the deadline.

Keep An Asset Register That Includes Depreciation

Know what you own, serial numbers and all. Most importantly, you need to know how much it is worth. This is a simple yet very effective step to take to know the real value of your business. Do it early on: it will save you much heartache and effort when it comes to meeting your tax obligations at the end of the financial year. After all, you must claim all the tax breaks you can get – they are there for the taking. It will also prove beneficial later on should you decide to sell your business.

Work With An External Accountant For Tax Planning

A good accountant will never cost you money; they will save it for you. However, make sure you are working with someone good. Make their job easier by providing them with as much up-to-date information as you can. This is where having good business systems will pay dividends.

Client Market Research

This vital area is invaluable in selecting the approach you will take with each target market and in presenting your business. Training your new team members in all the facets of how you currently conduct your client market research will be invaluable to their success. Map out the significant characteristics and methods you employ that have been highly successful for you.

Have A System For Payroll & Superannuation

It should not take you long at all if you are following a simple and easy-to-use system. You could consider outsourcing this function.

From an employee's point-of-view, this is what it is all about. Nothing will upset them as much as not depositing their salaries or wages on time. A late payment can cause untold inconvenience, not to mention cost and embarrassment, as automatic deductions could default and penalties be incurred.

Remember, employees trade time for money. They have put in the time, now you need to ensure your side of the deal is honoured.

Life Time Value Of Customers

Understanding the real value your customers represent to your business over the years they deal with you is important. If your average sale per customer is $75 and you think of that customer as having a $75 value to your business, you are underestimating their true worth. For example, if a customer spends $75 on average every time they purchase from you, but the average number of times they buy from you is four times per year, and they will be buying that product for a span of 10 years, their lifetime value is $3000. How much in dollar profit is that customer worth to your business? How much would it cost to keep a current customer coming back? It is often far less expensive to keep a customer coming back than it is to attract new customers.

Acquisition Cost Of Customers

How much does it cost you in advertising dollars to generate a customer? Through a simple "Break Even Analysis" procedure you will know how cost effective your efforts are. Your goal is to acquire customers at the lowest possible cost; preferably reaching a point that every dollar spent on marketing produces a profit. You will have an unlimited marketing budget at this point.

80/20 Analysis

This is an extremely powerful tool that can be used in all facets of your business as well as in your personal life. Many of us are familiar with the idea that 20% of our product or service produces 80% of our sales. Do you realize that this imbalance occurs throughout all areas of business and life in general? Consider wealth for example – only a small minority of people controls the vast majority of the wealth. Through application of the 80/20 principle, you can drastically change the performance of your business. Consider the way in which a major supermarket is merchandised: successful retailers know which 20% of their products generate 80% of their sales, but they also know which 20% of their products generate 80% of their profits and use this information very effectively.

Delivery And Distribution

Do What You Do In Full On Time Every Time

Run Paperless Systems

If you can run it via the computer and can avoid handling documents in triplicate, you will save a mountain of time.

You will also save heaps of money. Paper is expensive, and so is storage space. Massive filing systems are difficult to manage and find documents in. They also need to be catalogued and expanded each year. Then there's archiving to be done every five years or so.

Electronic systems are easy to set up and manage. Data needs to be backed up regularly and stored off site. Specialist firms can take care of this area cost effectively and without fuss. On the other hand, you can do it yourself.

Deliver Your Service With Systematic Consistency

If there is a way to make great service happen time after time, then make sure your people are using it.

It is no use having a great system if nobody uses it, or if people only use it from time to time. The key to developing loyal customers through service delivery is to be consistent. It does not matter at what level you deliver the service; it has to be consistent to make an impression.

People like to know what to expect. They find comfort in the familiar.

Change Product Packaging For Safer Delivery

If you are getting broken items, then maybe it will cost less to repackage.

Repackaging can also provide an opportunity to re-launch a product or to reposition it. Going up market could justify an increase in price. Either way, repackaging could increase your bottom line.

Reorganize Stock According To Highest Turnover

Make it easy on yourself. Everything that sells a lot should be easy to get to.

Think of rearranging your storeroom or warehouse. Not only will it be easier to manage, it will act as a visible sales barometer – your team will be able to see just how fast the stock is moving.

Simplify Your Order Pick & Pack Process

If it is less time consuming to put away and then distribute stock, you will save a bundle.
The name of the game is to avoid duplication of effort. Labour costs are time-related, so draw up a flow chart of your distribution process to see if you can save time by simplifying your systems.

Forecast Stock Movements

By forecasting, you will always know what to order, when to order it and what money you will have to spend.

Inventory control is all about timing and knowing your business. Running out of stock can cost your business in lost sales. It can also cost you a customer.

On the other hand, having too much stock ties up capital unnecessarily. By having a good record-keeping system, you will be able to forecast stock movement so you can place replenishment orders in time to ensure optimum use of capital and maintain sufficient levels of stock.

Complete A Purchasing & Stock Receiving System

Make sure you only order what is needed, pay a good price for it, and make sure you get what you pay for.

If you make your purchases and receive stock in a haphazard fashion, chances are some orders will cost you more than they should. Develop a system to ensure uniformity based on carefully considered guidelines. That way there will be less chance for human error or impulsive buying costing you money. A good stock receiving system will also ensure mistakes made by your suppliers are picked up before the items are booked into stock. This will save you the added expense of retrieving these items and returning them for refunds or replacement, as well as the consequent losses that could be incurred through not having the item available for sale.

Outsource Logistics & Warehouse Support

Specialist companies are often much better than you are at warehousing and distribution.

They have the expertise and experience and can deliver far less expensive services than you could by doing it in-house. This option allows you to concentrate on your core competencies by freeing up capital that could be diverted into other areas of your business. Warehouses, storerooms, forklift trucks, and dedicated logistics and warehouse personnel are all expensive. Can you do without the hassles and save by outsourcing?

Outsource All Delivery Of Purchases

Stop paying for delivery vans and things you do not need. Have a specialist company handle it for you.
Transport is one of the single most expensive items for any company when you take into account the cost of purchasing and running a delivery fleet. Fuel, tires, servicing and insurance might cost more than they are worth to you.

Complete Regular Stock Takes

Make sure you know what you have and be sure to use that information wisely.

If you do not know what you have got in stock, how would you know what profit you are making? Remember, Profit Is King. Managing your cash flow is the name of the game. Having cash tied up in stock you do not know about is costly. It also affects your stock ordering system, the cost of storage and whether or not you have shrinkage. You could also be incurring unnecessary losses due to product passing its use-by date.

Quantify Service Or Product Delivery Costs

Know how much you are spending so you can look for ways to improve and systematize.

By conducting an in-depth study into the actual

delivery cost to your business, you can decide whether or not the cost is justified. By putting these costs under the spotlight, you may very well streamline your system by cutting out duplication and inefficiencies. At the very least, you will come up with a more efficient system that is cost-effective. You may decide that the best option is to outsource. Either way, you will now have a far better understanding, and control, of these costs.

Measure Quality & Professionalism Of Service Delivery

The more you measure it, the better it gets. It is a simple step.

By keeping the quality of your service delivery operation under the spotlight, you are sure to improve its level of professionalism. However, you need to ensure you have a good measurement system in place. By constantly measuring quality and professionalism, you would also be constantly improving the delivery system, which in turn will improve the performance of the relevant team members. Their professionalism will increase, their jobs will get easier and they will perform better.

Follow Up & Measure Quality & Time Of Delivery

Your customers love on-time, quality delivery, so make sure they are getting it.

When it comes to business, the quality of your delivery service can make it or break it. It is no use delivering an item that is damaged on route to your customer. It is also no good delivering a purchase later than when it was promised.

By taking some simple steps to ensure this aspect of your customer experience is not found wanting, you will be going a long way to ensuring repeat business.

Measurement Systems For Freight, Couriers & Vehicles

Getting it there the first time, on time, saves everyone a lot of time and money.

This is one area that lends itself to systematization. Many good transportation systems exist, so if you cannot develop your own, buy one. Monitoring the effectiveness of your current system, whether it is formal or informal, will highlight areas for improvement. It may even indicate outsourcing would be more efficient and cost effective.

Not only will going through this exercise save you money, it will ensure your customers remain happy with your service. It will also go a long way to ensuring they do business with you again.

Measure and Use Re-order Levels

Never order before you have to and never run out of stock.

This may sound obvious, but ordering before you have to not only ties up capital in unnecessary stock and storage space, it also uses limited cash resources. You need to monitor stock movements to time reorders so they arrive just on time. Conversely, you must ensure you never run out of stock, because this could not only cost you a sale, it could cost you a customer for good. That customer might be forced to buy from your competitor, find he is happy with their product and service, strike up a relationship and stay.

Use An Order Tracking System

Make sure every order is traceable, and then if anything disappears you can start tracking it down. Things do go wrong from time-to-time, and deliveries do go astray. Losing a delivery may not seem to be a problem on its own, but understanding the cause can help you ensure it does not happen again. It could help tighten up or fine-tune your delivery system.

If an order does get lost, and your client finds you instituted an efficient recovery or tracking system, any potentially damaging consequences could be turned into positive outcomes. You could salvage a good customer and the deal.

Deploy Staff For Service Delivery

Know your busy times and roster your team accordingly.

There is nothing worse, from a customer's point-of-view, than having to wait at the checkout when there are several unattended checkouts. Redeploying staff to speed up service delivery during busy times is far easier and less costly than having to cope with inefficiencies. It could cost you more than sales – it could cost you customers.

Increase Security

Stock damage and loss is often not a priority, but you have to make sure it is not happening.

Stock shrinkage, pilfering and theft are avoidable. They are an unnecessary factor that can too easily get out of hand if left unchecked. Increased security can also have the added benefit of increasing staff morale and customer satisfaction. It might be the smartest investment you make.

Confirm Details Before Service Or Product Delivery

Having to redo an order or resend it has to be the fastest way to bankrupt your business.

Stupid errors like getting the wrong delivery address or the wrong town could prove very costly. Not only could orders get lost and cost you money, but they could also be delivered to the wrong address and accepted there. In this case, you would have to bear the loss and resend the order. Your customers would be most unhappy, especially if the orders were urgently needed. They might decide to change to a competitor.

Institute a system that double checks delivery address details – a simple fix for a potentially expensive problem.

Use A 'Just In Time' Stock Delivery System

This system makes sure you not only get the stock, but also get it just before it is needed.

Efficiency in this area can save you a fortune.

Inefficiency here can cost you your business. It is all about careful monitoring and forecasting. It is the ideal scenario for a computer-based system.

Your Business Action Plan

Action Plan – Mastery Level

Priority	Strategy	Individual Responsible	Investment	Start Date	Completion Date

Priority	Strategy	Individual Responsible	Investment	Start Date	Completion Date
	Profit Margin				
High-Moderate-Low	Increase Your Margins/Prices				
High-Moderate-Low	Sell More Big Margin Goods/Services				
High-Moderate-Low	NO Discounting				
High-Moderate-Low	Sell Only Quality				
High-Moderate-Low	Sell Your Own Label				
High-Moderate-Low	Sell An Exclusive Label				
High-Moderate-Low	Sell Via Direct Mail/Internet				
High-Moderate-Low	Sell Via Party Plan/Internet				
High-Moderate-Low	Keep An Accurate Database				
High-Moderate-Low	Commission Only Sales Team				
High-Moderate-Low	Provide Team Training				
High-Moderate-Low	Pay NO Overtime				
High-Moderate-Low	Reduce Team Size				
High-Moderate-Low	Reduce Unnecessary Management				
High-Moderate-Low	Reduce Directors Fees				
High-Moderate-Low	Efficiency, Productivity & Time Management				
High-Moderate-Low	Negotiate Employment Agreements				
High-Moderate-Low	Team Incentives Based On Margins				

Priority	Strategy	Individual Responsible	Investment	Start Date	Completion Date
High-Moderate-Low	Reduce Duplication				
High-Moderate-Low	Know Your Actual Costs				
High-Moderate-Low	Work Costs As A Percentage of Sales				
High-Moderate-Low	Set Monthly Expenditure Budgets				
High-Moderate-Low	Allow Your Team To Buy Only With An Authorized Purchase Order				
High-Moderate-Low	Better Negotiation Skills				
High-Moderate-Low	Reduce ALL Costs By 10%				
High-Moderate-Low	Do It Right The First Time				
High-Moderate-Low	Recycle				
High-Moderate-Low	Decrease Range				
High-Moderate-Low	Take Stock On Consignment				
High-Moderate-Low	Lower $$ Tied Up In Inventory				
High-Moderate-Low	Sell Only Fast Moving Stock				
High-Moderate-Low	Buy In Bulk, Pay & Receive Over Time				
High-Moderate-Low	Manufacture Yourself				
High-Moderate-Low	Repackage Smaller/Own Label				
High-Moderate-Low	Promote Idle Time				
High-Moderate-Low	Rent Idle Space				
High-Moderate-Low	Work Two Or Even Three Shifts				

Priority	Strategy	Individual Responsible	Investment	Start Date	Completion Date
High-Moderate-Low	Have Smaller Outlets				
High-Moderate-Low	Work From Home				
High-Moderate-Low	Have A Mobile Business				
High-Moderate-Low	Join/Start A Buying Group				
High-Moderate-Low	Re-finance				
High-Moderate-Low	Charge For A Finance Facility				
High-Moderate-Low	30 Day Terms To 7 Days				
High-Moderate-Low	Invest In Technology				
High-Moderate-Low	Systematize The Routine, Humanize The Exceptions				
High-Moderate-Low	Automate As Much As Possible				
High-Moderate-Low	Sell Obsolete Equipment/Machinery				
High-Moderate-Low	Reduce/Eliminate Taxation Expense				
High-Moderate-Low	Negotiate Fixed Not Variable Expense				
High-Moderate-Low	Employ People In House				
High-Moderate-Low	Outsource				
High-Moderate-Low	Use A Company Card For Bonus Points & Up To 55 Days Interest Free				
High-Moderate-Low	Rent For Maximum Tax Write Off				
High-Moderate-Low	Change Accountants				
High-Moderate-Low	Keep Overheads To A Minimum				

Priority	Strategy	Individual Responsible	Investment	Start Date	Completion Date
High-Moderate-Low	Stop Running Ads That Do Not Work				
High-Moderate-Low	Measure Everything				
High-Moderate-Low	Regular/Timely Accounts				
High-Moderate-Low	Get Phone Bills Etc. Checked				

	Testing & Measuring				
High-Moderate-Low	Complete & Keep To Monthly & Yearly Budgets				
High-Moderate-Low	Measure Conversion Rate for Each Sales Person				
High-Moderate-Low	Keep A Record Of Your Profit Margins				
High-Moderate-Low	Complete A Petty Cash System				
High-Moderate-Low	Complete A Purchasing System For All Internal Purchases				
High-Moderate-Low	Always Complete A Marketing Campaign Profit Analysis				
High-Moderate-Low	Continuously Measure The Number & Origin of All Leads				
High-Moderate-Low	Constantly Monitor Credit Control & The Age Of Your Accounts				
High-Moderate-Low	Measure Your Average Dollar Sale For Every Team Member				
High-Moderate-Low	Record The Number Of Transactions For Each Customer				
High-Moderate-Low	Complete A Monthly Balance Sheet				
High-Moderate-Low	Measure Key Performance Indicators In All Areas Of The Company				
High-Moderate-Low	Complete A Weekly Bank Reconciliation				

Priority	Strategy	Individual Responsible	Investment	Start Date	Completion Date
High-Moderate-Low	Daily Or Weekly Update Your Cash Flow Statements				
High-Moderate-Low	Have A Daily Banking System				
High-Moderate-Low	Complete Regular Stock Control Check Ups				
High-Moderate-Low	Complete All Regular Government Returns				
High-Moderate-Low	Keep An Asset Register That Includes Depreciation				
High-Moderate-Low	Work With An External Accountant For Tax Planning				
High-Moderate-Low	Client Market Research				
High-Moderate-Low	Have A System For Payroll & Superannuation				
High-Moderate-Low	Life Time Value Of Customers				
High-Moderate-Low	Acquisition Cost Of Customers				
High-Moderate-Low	80/20 Analysis				

Priority	Strategy	Individual Responsible	Investment	Start Date	Completion Date
High-Moderate-Low	**Delivery & Distribution**				
High-Moderate-Low	Run Paperless Systems				
High-Moderate-Low	Deliver Your Service With Systematic Consistency				
High-Moderate-Low	Change Product Packaging For Safer Delivery				
High-Moderate-Low	Reorganize Stock According To Highest Turnover				
High-Moderate-Low	Simplify Your Order Pick & Pack Process				
High-Moderate-Low	Forecast Stock Movements				

Priority	Strategy	Individual Responsible	Investment	Start Date	Completion Date
High-Moderate-Low	Complete A Purchasing & Stock Receiving System				
High-Moderate-Low	Outsource Logistics & Warehouse Support				
High-Moderate-Low	Outsource All Delivery Of Purchases				
High-Moderate-Low	Complete Regular Stock Takes				
High-Moderate-Low	Quantify Service Or Product Delivery Costs				
High-Moderate-Low	Measure Quality & Professionalism Of Service Delivery				
High-Moderate-Low	Follow Up & Measure Quality & Time Of Delivery				
High-Moderate-Low	Measurement Systems For Freight, Couriers & Vehicles				
High-Moderate-Low	Measure and Use Re-order Levels				
High-Moderate-Low	Use An Order Tracking System				
High-Moderate-Low	Deploy Staff For Service Delivery				
High-Moderate-Low	Increase Security				
High-Moderate-Low	Confirm Details Before Service Or Product Delivery				
High-Moderate-Low	Use A 'Just In Time' Stock Delivery System				

ABOUT THE AUTHOR

John Millar is the Managing Director, Senior Business Coach Trainer and Consultant with More Profit Less Time Pty Ltd and CEO-ONDEMAND. Along with his many other business interests, John is proud to have been an associate of the most successful coaching team in the world.

He is recognized as a global leader and has been benchmarked against over 1,300 colleagues in 31 countries. John has over 25 years of hands-on ownership, management, coaching, and entrepreneurial experience in a broad range of industry sectors, including retail, wholesale, import, export, IT, trades and trade services, automotive, primary production, food services, transport, manufacturing, mining, professional services, the fitness industry, and more.

He has extensive experience developing and providing training for small to medium-sized companies and a variety of publicly listed corporate companies. John is an accomplished and talented public and professional speaker. He has been a mentor working with sales/management activities for businesses with a turnover under $100,000 per annum, over $100 million turnover, and everything in between, with great success.

John currently works with business owners and their teams across Australia and has a "Whatever it takes" attitude that has enabled him to help his clients grow their business profits by up to 800%.

 If you are ready to be coached by one of the best in the business, register at:

www.ceo-ondemand.com.au

Make sure to visit www.moreprofitlesstime.com for the new online Management Development Program: The Business Essentials Series.

CEOONDEMAND

ACCLAIM FOR JOHN MILLAR'S

Business Coaching and Training in their own words...

"Without John Millar as my Business Coach I wouldn't have a business today."—Grant Jennings Managing Director, Jigsaw Projects

"Taking the decision to be coached and trained by John Millar was carefully considered after experiencing those who over promised and under delivered. I am pleased to say the content of his courses are the tools we all need to master as business owners. His delivery is engaging, thought provoking and empowering and after every session I came away re-energised. John always makes himself available for business building advice both via Skype and face to face beyond the scope of delivery. With his extensive personal experience in building small businesses, he knows and understands what it takes to establish and grow a business.I have no hesitation endorsing John Millar as an educator and business coach and the bonus is he is a very nice person."— Anne Lederman Managing Director FB Salons"

Johns training with my management team was excellent, it was very different from the business coaching and support I have had in the past. John was clear, thoughtful and he addressed the issues we needed to cover without us even knowing they were being addressed! His follow up has been fantastic and exactly what I needed. I would recommend John and his team to anyone looking at getting some business coaching and training done" —Wendy Crawford, Peopleworx

"In my dealings with John as our business coach, I have found him to be a motivated and insightful agent of positive change. He is able to burrow down to the root cause of issues and introduce effective forms of measurement. John then identifies and implements practical solutions and is there to provide the gentle persuasion required to ensure that results are achieved." —Mark Felton, Lindale Insurances

"You have coached and trained us so well throughout the year that we are now used to & find it easy to prepare a 90 day plan, then breaks it down to actionable bite size pieces. Planning in business & personal life certainly is important. It allows us to identify the important things & the bigger picture. Thank you for your support & guidance throughout the year. And not to mention your insight, external perspective to review & assist our business moving forward." —Linda Turner, Director Roy A McDonald Certified Practicing Accountants

"If you want to achieve sales results you never thought were possible and give yourself a competitive edge my strong suggestion is to engage John services and listen closely to what John has to say, during the time I was trained by John I was one of eight sales consultants in a national business for 10 out of the 13 months I lead the sales tally and in 1 quarter I generated three times the revenue of the national sales force combined. Johns training and experience was well worth the investment and paid big dividends. Thanks John." —Julian Fadini, Bellvue Capital

"John is a very enthusiastic trainer and business coach, he is very passionate about getting business owners and their team where they need to be. He goes the extra mile to keep ahead of the latest developments which he then uses to benefit his clients." —Darren Reddy CPA

"I have been to a few seminars and heard John speak numerous times about sales, marketing and business. He is a very knowledgeable and extremely enthusiastic business coach in all his interactions and I would recommend him to all business owners who need a sales and marketing boost!" —Andrew Heath, Managing Director, Fresh Living Group

"I worked with John Millar and found his business knowledge, passion and innovation to be inspiring.

He has always been able to set (and achieve) strategic long and short-term goals both for himself and his clients without losing that personal connection he builds with everyone he meets. He has been and I believe will continue to be a strong mentor and trainer for anyone wanting to take that next step in their business." —Bree Webster, Online Marketing Guru

"Massive Action Day" – what an understatement, John Millar's 4 hour frenzy challenged me to seriously review areas of my business I would not have gone to .... In this way, the process identified incongruence's in my mind, my business and my modus operandi. It's created a paradigm shift. Thanks John, the road map just got a whole lot clearer. Your friendship and insights since 2003 have been a gift to my business and I." —Andrew Reay, Counsellor, Hypnotherapist and Counsellor, Thinkshift Transformations

"John Millar is not your usual Business coach or trainer; he gets involved with you and your business and provides hands on help to make sure you follow through on his advice. He is highly motivated to help his clients and his personal guarantee certainly shows this. He has now transposed his thoughts, advice and love of good business onto a series of DVD's in his business venture – More Profit Less Time. This has excellent tips and advice for anyone either starting out or already in business. I highly recommend John to any business owner who wants to run a business and not a j.o.b.!" —Darren Cassidy, Managing Director HR2U

"I and many of my Business Partners and colleagues have worked with John since 2010 as our business oath, trainer and motivator and found him to be an extremely motivational person to assist us achieve our business goals. This company and its products allows for John's skill set to be accessed by a wider number of potential clients. His very professional DVD series is extremely good value for money and is easily accessible for all of us who are time poor. If you are looking to maximise your and your business's results and to start achieving your goals and dreams, contact John; you won't look back!!" —Mark Cleland, Mortgage Choice

"John develops real relationships with the people he comes into contact with. He is passionate about what he does. His DVD and group training series, is full of good ideas and process to make your business better. Knowing what to do and actually doing it are two different things. John is excellent at helping you get things done." —Carey Rudd, Sales Director, Online Knowledge

"I have known John since 2004 and found him to be extremely knowledgably in both Sales and Business systems as a business coach without peer. John has provided me with business advice as well as personal coaching over the years, helping me with the running of my organisation. I'm impressed with John's DVD series where he has condensed a lot of the information in an easy to follow format that any business owner can use immediately. I wish he had released these DVDs earlier, as they are a goldmine of information, and practical how to that allow anyone to increase the profit in their business and get back valuable wasted time." —Steve Psaradellis, Managing Director, TEBA

"John's DVD and workbook delivery of his no-nonsense advice provides a low-cost option for those business owners looking to set and achieve goals that will increase profit. I found the conversational style of the DVD's easy to follow, whilst the requirement to pause the DVD and write down some action points ensured a level of commitment to the advice being provided." —Mark Felton, Lindale Insurances

"I only met John briefly at a BNI meeting and knew instantly i need to hire him for my business as my business coach. His attitude towards work and how to improve my cash line had an instant effect on before, even before I finally hired him on an official basis. I found myself thinking "what would John do" and this was only after just meeting him. I cannot see my business expend and give me "More Profit Less Time" without John's expert direction and training. If you want to succeed in business life, you need John Millar, without him you're just kidding yourself " —Leslie Cachia, Managing Director, Letac Drafting

"I can highly recommend John Millar to any business owner who wants to grow his business. When I hear very positive feedback from colleagues who are skeptics by nature about John's ability and skills, I know John will help all those he comes in contact with. John comes with a selfless nature and the willingness to work inside a client's business to make it succeed. Rare indeed!" —Darren Cassidy, Managing Director, HR2U"I first met John Millar in mid-2010 and have always found him to be of an honest and generous character that engenders an easy association with him. I love how easy he is to listen to and how passionate he is about his work and topics. John demonstrates a love for life and his work and I have no hesitation in recommending his services." —Kathie M Thomas, Managing Director, VA

"I have listened to John speak on a number of occasions and find him a very knowledgeable speaker with a passion for what he does. I have also interacted with a number of his clients and they all tell me that he helps them achieve results in their business. If you are looking for business help John is a person you can trust." —Carey Rudd, Sales Director, Online Knowledge

"John knows his stuff, he knows how the get results, John has so many great ideas in building a business and helping business owners work less and make more money. John has released a DVD set on doing just that. I have watched the 1st one and it was great, very informative and easy to understand, I happily recommend John to anyone in need of help and guidance" —Frank Eramo, Proprietor, Dynotune

"I have known John only for a short time, however the impact that he has had on me, not just my business has helped me to visualise opportunities that I began to doubt my ability to realise. He is encouraging and at the same time challenging so that he can/you can, begin to see how to maximise the business potential, John calls it being an unreasonable friend, I call it being a mate. If you have any questions about the direction of your business, if you want to seem your bottom line improve not just turnover but real profit, if you want a person who will work with you then I strongly recommend that you engage him at your earliest convenience. John is the best thing that has happened to my business. I could tell you about the way he is on track to make

1/2 a million for me on his contacts alone, but that actually sells him short, he has become like my partner in business, and cares about my success as if it was his own, we will flourish because I took the step to employ his training to help me grow. If you get a chance to get him training you, don't wait like I did, get in as quickly as possible, his time is your business and if like me your business is to make money, then every day you don't have him on retainer you lose money." —Russell Summers, Managing Director, The Give Life Centre

"It's usually easy to be mediocre in business but it's impossible when you have John Millar training you. He has been my right hand since 2003!" —David Manser, CFO, Hydrosteer

"I now have a commercial, profitable business and now it's my choice when I work IN my business and when I work ON it and have had john helping me in business since 1988. I can't imagine not having John as a part of our business." —David Wall, Director, D&K Transport

"The work John has done since 2008 coaching and training our marketing team, administration and finance teams, buyers, store managers and staff nationally have been fantastic." —Ross Sudano, Director, Anaconda Adventure Stores

"John is a creative, professional, practical and committed business coach and trainer. His approach since we first met him in 1994 to working with a client team through the application of useful tools, information and anecdotes along with his easy going & easy to understand delivery sets him apart from

other business coaches that I have used in the past."
—Anthony Beasley, Director, The Astra Group

"I have worked with John Millar for the since 2004 and I didn't think it was possible to achieve what we have achieved together. His business coaching, training and services just get better and better!" — Terrance Chong, Managing Director, Echo Graphics and Printing

"John's business coaching, training and support has transformed our business across Australia and New Zealand since 2008."—rose vis, managing director, VIP Australia

"We first met John in 2005, he is AMAZING at sales, marketing, operations, logistics, finance training and so much more. Since engaging John as our business coach our business has exploded, our team are happy, our clients are raving about us and my husband and I now take at least 12 weeks holidays a year, EVERY year." —Shirley Du, Director, Goldline Technology

"It's the no nonsense results driven business coaching and training focus John bought to the table that had such a massive effect on our business." — David Runkel, Director, Tracomp Fabrication and Steel

"We started working with John in early 2010, within 90 days of working with and being trained by John Millar we had the biggest and most profitable month in our 15 year history. That's impressive." —Hugh Gilchrist, Managing Director, Australian Moulding Company

"If you don't have John as your business trainer you aren't meeting your business potential." —Don Robertson, Director, Medallion Electrical Services

Thank You!

www.ingramcontent.com/pod-product-compliance
Lightning Source LLC
Chambersburg PA
CBHW060414190526
45169CB00002B/897